The Manners
of the Dervishes

The Manners of the Dervishes

TALES FROM THE GULESTAN

Saadi
Translated from the Persian
by
Charles David Kimbrell

ISBN: 1514294176
ISBN 13: 9781514294178
Library of Congress Control Number: 2015909571
CreateSpace Independent Publishing Platform
North Charleston, South Carolina

About the Author: Charles Kimbrell has a degree in Ancient Near Eastern History and Archeology from the University of California at Berkeley. On September 11, 2001, after watching an airliner crash into the World Trade Center on television, he decided to dedicate his life to improving communication and understanding between the people of the United States and the Muslim world.

E-mail: CDKimbrell@sbcglobal.net
Twitter: @CDKimbrell

About the Illustrator: Emily Espinosa is an artist and award winning cartoon animator. She lives in the hills of northern California with her dog, listening to funny songs and is a big fan of cute things.

E-mail: catsgomeow@riseup.net

Acknowledgments

THERE IS NO WAY I could have translated Saadi and made his work available in English without the help of my teacher, Nahid Bibehani, who has patiently taught me both modern and classical Persian. I would also like to thank Masoud Delejani, a modern Persian poet, for his advice on translating some of the poems. Irshad Alam, a sheikh of the Naqshbandi-Mujaddidi Sufi path, has also helped by teaching me both Sufi philosophy and practice. I would especially like to thank my dear wife, Suzanne Skrivanich, for her encouragement and help and also for editing my final draft.

Charles David Kimbrell, Berkeley 2015

Introduction

THE *MANNERS OF DERVISHES* IS part of *The Gulestan (Flower Garden)*, published in 1258 by Mushariffudin bin Muslihuddin Abdullah, more popularly known as Saadi. Born in Shiraz, a city in western Iran, he is one of the most popular poets in Persian literature.

For hundreds of years, the entire Muslim world was ruled by the caliphs of Baghdad, successors to the Prophet Muhammad. By Saadi's time, the caliphs had little direct control. The various kings and sultans reigning over these lands paid homage to the caliph and maintained a semblance of unity but ruled without interference.

Shiraz at that time was a collection of houses and public buildings built of stone or mud brick surrounded by a wall. Traders came with caravans of camels carrying goods from as far away as China. Individual houses were built around a courtyard. If the house was big enough, the courtyard would have a fountain and a garden. During the summer months, people spent their days and nights on the roofs, where they could catch a cool breeze.

Women of the wealthier families rarely went out of the house. The nobility of the family was reflected in the chastity of its women. Families took extraordinary efforts to protect themselves from the hint of a scandal by ensuring that women would never be seen by strange men. As a result, the women spent their lives in houses, doing needlework, weaving carpets and looking out of latticework windows on the upper stories.

In one of the stories in this collection, *My Father*, Saadi described reading the *Qur'an* with his father late at night. Saadi was comfortable writing in both Persian and Arabic and had the honor of being one of the few educated people in his society.

Schooling was for boys and focused on learning to read and memorize religious texts. The schools themselves (*madrassa*, in Arabic) were appended to a mosque or other religious institution. The boys sat on the floor in a carpeted room, placed their *Qur'ans* on low wooden stands to keep them elevated over their feet and chanted the sacred words aloud. In addition to the *Qur'an*, students learned other texts such as the *Hadith*, or sayings of the Prophet Muhammad. For more advanced study, some students might learn the teachings of Aristotle or other Greek philosophers, which had been translated into Arabic and which have continued to enjoy wide popularity in the Muslim world.

Saadi described the moment when he decided to write the *Gulestan*. He was sitting in a garden, possibly in Shiraz, with one of his disciples admiring the beautiful flowers.

Saadi remarked, "The wise have said, 'What does not last is not worthy of attachment.'"

"What must be done?" the disciple asked.

"For the delight of onlookers and the enjoyment of those present," Saadi said. "I can compose a book called the *Gulestan*. The cold winds of autumn will not damage its pages[1]. In it, the springtime of love and beauty will never change.

---

1 The word for leaf and page, "*warak*" is the same in Persian.

"Of what use to you is a real flower?
Take a leaf from my Flower Garden.
A flower lasts only five or six days.
The Flower Garden is always fresh."

Saadi then began to dictate the *Gulestan.*

Saadi identified himself as a dervish. The word "dervish" (*darvish*, in Persian) means threshold of a door. When Saadi used this term, he was referring to a mystic, a portal between the mundane and the spiritual worlds. Saadi often used the word "Sufi" (*safa* or *suf*, in Arabic) meaning the pure or undyed wool cloth worn by dervishes, to mean the same thing. In modern times, writers in English use the word "Sufism" to describe the movement as a whole while they use the words "dervish" and "Sufi" to refer to individual practitioners.

By Saadi's time, large numbers of people in the Muslim world identified as Sufis. Sufism is a blend of Islam and pre-Islamic traditions. Syria had been Christian. The Turks practiced Shamanism. Afghanistan and India were Buddhist.[2] The populations of these countries combined their new faith with beliefs and practices from before the Islamic conquest developing a rich blend.

By becoming a dervish, Saadi renounced any claim to family status or property. Dervishes lived an ascetic life like the Buddhist and Christian monks of pre-Islamic Afghanistan and Syria. Saadi's decision made it possible for him to see the world. He wrote of making the pilgrimage, or Hajj, to Mecca in Arabia and of visiting Syria and Lebanon. During his travels, he met with a wide variety of people and wrote poems about them. These poems, combined with short descriptions and stories, express themes such as the importance of kindness, the superiority

---

2 Arberry, A.J., *Sufism: an Account of the Mystics of Islam* (London: Allen and Unwin) 1950, p. 11.

of contentment, and the problems arising from a zealous adherence to outward forms of religion.

In Saadi's time, Sufis were the driving force behind classical Persian poetry. As A.J. Arberry in his book, *Sufism: an Account of the Mystics of Islam*, writes:

> If Sufism had given birth to nothing more than a lofty ethic and a subtle metaphysic, it might have been allowed that the movement had made a substantial contribution to human thought and experience. But when Sufism gripped the mind and soul of Iran, and the abounding poetic imagination of the Persians discovered this new theatre to display itself, Islamic Mysticism developed aesthetically in a manner soaring high above the ranges of pure speculation. Classical Persian poetry is to a very notable extent Sufi in content and inspiration.[3]

The Persians took Sufi philosophy and applied it to the mundane world by use of stories, anecdotes, fables, and poems addressing real-life issues. Saadi's work fits into this tradition. He wrote about criminals in such stories as *The Dervish Thief* or *The Burglar*. In *Music*, he explored what happens when people listen to a bad musician. In *Guts*, he related a story about a sheikh who passes gas in public. Throughout his work, he focused on applying Sufi philosophy to the challenges and contradictions of everyday life. By doing so, he taught people to adapt the abstractions of Sufi philosophy to the mundane world.

Saadi's work has been popular in the Persian speaking world ever since his lifetime. Adaptations of his stories and poems have been used in textbooks for children. Modern Iranians, Tadjiks, Afghans, and Pakistanis often quote him. Rumi and Omar Khayyam are popular in English translations. Now, it is time to make Saadi's literature available in English.

---

3 *Ibid*, p.106.

Characters

DIFFERENT CHARACTERS APPEAR OVER AND over in Saadi's stories. Some of these people are solitary mystics who live in the wilds. He called them "hermits"(*parsi*, in Persian).

Saadi often pointed out the differences between the mystical dervishes and practitioners of orthodox Islam, whom he called "devotees"(*abed*, in Arabic). A devotee focuses on the outer representations of religion and may object to the mystical practices of the dervishes. Saadi called devotees who go to extremes "zealots" (*zahir*, in Arabic).[4]

The most enigmatic people Saadi wrote about are "masters of their hearts"(*sahib dil*, in Persian). These people have developed the ability to read gut feelings or emotions and are able to see through the hypocrisy and foolishness of others. In some ways, they are the most enlightened of Saadi's characters.

---

4 The Islamic State of Iraq and Syria (ISIS) is an extreme example of modern zealot ideology.

The Stories

STORY 1

Outside and Inside

ONE OF THE GREAT ONES was asked about a hermit whom others had been demeaning.

He answered, "I see nothing wrong about his outside, and I know of nothing wrong about his inside."

> *If you see plain clothing,*
> *Assume the person is good.*
> *You want to know his inner thoughts,*
> *Don't be the policeman of his soul.*

A Tyrant and a Fool

I SAW A DERVISH WITH his head down on the threshold of the *Ka'aba*[5] wailing and saying, "O forgiving merciful one. You know what comes from a tyrant and a fool."[6]

> *I bring presents of guilt and transgression,*
> *I do not have obedience or trust.*
> *Sinners have regret for their sins,*
> *Wise people repent out of duty.*

Worshipers want retribution for their sins, and merchants want money for goods. I, who am a servant of God, bring hope and not repentance. As a beggar, and not as a merchant, I hope.

> *About the Ka'aba I saw a beggar,*
> *Who said, as he cried to himself,*
> *"I cannot say if my worship will be accepted,*
> *He is the one who will forgive my sins."*

---

5 The *Ka'aba* in Mecca is a stone building that all Muslims face during prayer. Pilgrims to Mecca circle the *Ka'aba* seven times as part of their pilgrimage.

6 This is a reference to a verse from the *Qur'an*, which says. "We have offered fidelity to the heavens and to the earth and to the mountains, but they shrank from it and were afraid, and man has taken it up, but he has become a tyrant and a fool." *Qur'an (33:72).* In other words, men in power often become tyrants and fools.

Abd Al Ghadar

ABD AL GHADAR GILANI, MAY the mercy of God be upon him. They saw him in the sanctuary of the Ka'aba with his head on the pavement.

He said. "O' God, please. If you always accept petitions, then I deserve to be heard. On the Day of Judgment, the blind and lame need not be shy about approaching you for forgiveness."

> *The return to the earth is nothing,*
> *Like a breeze that blows at dawn,*
> *Which I can never forget.*
> *Can he who is nothing come into the mind of man?*

STORY 4

The Burglar

A BURGLAR CAME INTO THE house of a hermit. He searched, but, there was nothing of value. Then he noticed the hermit had placed a sleeping mat so he could not leave without passing it.

> *I have heard that people with God's spirit*
> *Do not distress their enemies' hearts.*
> *How can one be so exalted?*
> *If he quarrels and wars with friends?*

Pure friendship is the same in your presence or absence. It is not some-one who says bad things behind your back and at the same time tells you he is willing to die for you.

> *Someone who greets you like a sheep,*
> *Then complains to you about others' faults,*
> *Is nothing but a man-eating wolf,*
> *When he is behind your back.*

Whoever brings before you the faults of others will surely carry your faults to others.

A Thief in Disguise

SOME DERVISHES WERE TRAVELING TOGETHER, and they shared among themselves both the good and the bad. I wanted to accompany them, but they wouldn't let me.

I said to them, "This is a new thing for the great ones to do, turning away from the company of ascetics and thereby miss something new. I am strong enough to help people and not hinder them."

> *One of them said to me,*
> > *"Don't let these words we say pierce your heart.*
> *A thief disguised as a dervish joined us a few days ago."*
> > *How can people know who a person is by his clothes?*
> *(Only) the writer knows what his book contains.*

As dervishes live in a state of trust, they were not suspicious and accepted him as a friend.

> *On the outside, the wise wear patched clothes.*
> > *This is enough to present to people.*
> *Act with righteousness and wear anything you want.*
> > *Put on a Sufi's crown and wear a flag.*[7]

---

7 It was the custom of Sufis to wear tall, felt hats and wear flags on their backs when going about asking for alms.

Abandoning the world, lust, and desire is sanctity.
Abandoning fine clothes is not.
Noble wrestlers wear only wrestling breeches,
And what use are weapons to one who won't fight.

"We traveled all day, and when night came we camped by a castle. The graceless thief took the jar we used to wash after relieving ourselves and went off to plunder."

A pretend saint,
Dressed like a Sufi,
Made the covering of the Ka'aba
Into the blanket of a donkey.

"After disappearing from the sight of the dervishes, the thief snuck into an inn and stole a jewelry box. By the next morning he was gone, and we were all thrown into prison. From that time on we decided to renounce the companionship of new people and stay by ourselves." As they say, safety in solitude.

When one of the tribe does something stupid,
Both the high and low are dishonored.
See how one wild bull from the countryside
Can make all the tame cattle in town look bad.

I said, "Thanks to God, the majestic and glorious, for I have not been deprived of the blessing of the dervishes' company. I have benefited by what you have told me, and this advice will be of use as people like me go through life."

One rude person in the assembly
Saddens the heart.
A whole basin of fine smelling rose water
Is ruined when a dirty dog jumps in.

Guest of a Sultan

A SUFI WAS ONCE THE guest of a sultan. While at dinner he ate less than he usually did. Afterwards, when they prayed, he prayed longer than he usually did in order to show the sultan just how pious he was.

> *O' Arab, you will never reach the Ka'aba,*
>> *Because you are on the road to Turkistan.*[8]

When the Sufi returned home, he asked to have food set out.

His son asked, "Father, didn't you eat anything at the sultan's dinner?"

The Sufi answered, "I didn't eat anything for a reason."

The son said, "If you need to eat again, then you should pray again too. Since you did both at the sultan's house for the same reason."

> *O' you, who show virtues on the palm of your hand,*
>> *And hide your faults in your armpit.*
> *Arrogant fool, what will you purchase*
>> *On the Day of Judgment with counterfeit money?*

---

8 In other words, you are going in the wrong direction.

My Father

I REMEMBER BEING PIOUS WHEN I was young, getting up at night to pray. One night I was sitting up with my father and holding the beloved *Qur'an* in my lap while the people around us were sleeping.

I said, "Not one of these people is getting up or praying. They are fast asleep as if they were dead."

My father answered, "My beloved son, right now I would rather you be asleep than sitting up and disparaging these people."

> *A pretender sees no one but himself,*
> *He has a veil in front of him.*
> *If he were blessed with God's all Seeing Eye,*
> *He would see no one is weaker than himself.*

Praising a Great Man

A GREAT MAN WAS BEING praised in an assembly. They praised his good qualities. He raised his head and said, "I am what I know myself to be."

> *In the eyes of the world I am good,*
> *My faults make me drop my head in shame.*
> *The peacock, praised for his beautiful tail,*
> *Is ashamed of his ugly feet.*

The Great Sheikh
of Lebanon

THERE WAS ONCE A GREAT sheikh of Lebanon. His piety, and the miracles he performed, were renowned through the land of the Arabs. He came into the great mosque at Damascus and was purifying himself at the fountain when he tripped and fell in the water. He almost drowned.

After prayers, one of the congregation came up and said. "I have a problem."

"What is it?" asked the sheikh.

The man continued, "I remember when the great sheikh walked on the surface of the African sea without his feet getting wet, and today he nearly drowned in shallow water. What happened?"

The great sheikh pondered for a while. He then raised his head and proclaimed. "Haven't you heard what the Holy Prophet said, 'I have time with Allah during which no angel or prophet is between us.' He did not say this was always the case. There were times when he was inspired by Gabriel and Michael. There were other times when he was satisfied with the company of Hafzi and Zaynab[9]. The vision of the righteous is between absolute clarity and obscurity."

---

9 Hafzi and Zaynab are women from the prophet's family.

Grief

SOMEONE ASKED A MAN WHO had lost his child, "O noble sir, you have smelled the odor of a fine Egyptian garment. Why don't you look for him in the well of Canaan?" [10]

The man replied, "My consciousness is like flashing tinder. One moment it appears, and then it is dark again. Sometimes I am sitting up in heaven. Sometimes I *feel so low that* I can't even see the back of my foot. Were a dervish to remain in this state, he would break down the division between the two worlds.[11]

---

10 This refers to the patriarch Jacob, who lost his beloved son Joseph after giving him a fine garment. Joseph's brothers became jealous and threw him down a well. Afterwards they sold him as a slave to the Egyptians for forty pieces of silver and told Jacob that Joseph had been killed by wild animals.

11 Derv`ishes believe that there are two worlds, the mundane and the spiritual.

The Sermon at Baalbeck

I GAVE A SERMON IN the assembly at Baalbeck.[12] I spoke a few words, but to a group whose hearts were withered and dead. I saw that they lived in a world of form, not a world of meaning. I realized that my spirit wasn't working, that my fire wasn't going to set wet wood alight. Then, I felt bad, like I was some sort of cattle driver, or even like someone holding a mirror for blind people. However, I had opened the door of meaning for some people.

I was giving a long explanation of the meaning of the verse "We are nearer to Him than the jugular vein."

When I said,

> *A friend is closer to me than I am myself,*
> *Why am I so far from him?*
> *What can I do?*
> *It is said that he is in my arms.*
> *But I am far from him.*

---

12 Baalbeck is a city in Lebanon.

These words had actually intoxicated me.[13] Like I was holding the dregs of the sermon in my hands. When a traveler passed by the crowd, it was as if the last cup of my sermon had intoxicated him. He began to shout, and others joined in. The crowd began to get wild.

"Thank God!" I said. "The people who are distant but listening are close, and those who are close but blind are really distant."

> *The listener who listens but does not understand*
> *Should not look at the speaker's face.*
> *Create a place of desire for one's beloved*
> *So the speaker may try that much harder.*

---

13 The *Qur'an* forbids drinking alcohol. Sufi poets, however, use the concept of intoxication and drinking wine as a metaphor for enlightenment.

Get Up

ONE NIGHT WHEN JOURNEYING TO Mecca, I became so tired that I was unable to walk. I lay down and told the camel driver to leave me alone.

> *How far can the feet of one who walks carry him,*
> *When a camel becomes exhausted by its load?*
> *You see the body of a fat person becoming thin,*
> *While the thin person dies of exhaustion.*

The camel driver said, "O brother, the sanctuary is before you and thieves are behind you. Get up and prosper or lie here and die."

> *It is nice to sleep under an acacia tree by the road.*
> *But, one must say good bye when it is time.*

The Tiger

I SAW A SUFI BY the ocean who had been mauled by a tiger. No medicine could relieve his pain, but he constantly thanked God, the noble and honorable.

They asked him why.

He answered. "Thank God that I have been injured, yet I have not injured others."

> *If my friend decides I must be slain.*
> *At that moment I will not grieve,*
> *Or say, what fault I have committed.*
> *I will grieve for offending others.*

The Dervish Thief

A DERVISH WHO HAD FALLEN into need stole a blanket from the house of a friend. The judge ordered his hand amputated, but the owner of the blanket interceded saying that he had approved of what the man had done.

The judge said. "You speak well, but I cannot ignore the law."

The blanket's owner said. "You speak the truth, but amputation is not applicable to one who takes things given to charity. I am a Sufi. Sufis own nothing, therefore everything in my house belongs to charity."

The judge released the thief, but only after telling him, "The world must be a very small place for you since you were stealing from the house of such a good friend."

The thief answered, "Haven't you heard the saying, 'Sweep out the house of a friend and don't knock at the door of an enemy.'"

> *Don't be helpless if you fall into need.*
> *Take your enemy's skins and your friend's furs.*

Forgetting God

A KING, UPON MEETING A Sufi, asked the Sufi if he thought about him when he wasn't around.

The Sufi replied. "I think about you whenever I forget God."

The one whom he drives from his door runs all over.
The one whom he calls to his door does not come.

Heaven and Hell

A PIOUS ONE DREAMT THAT he saw a king in heaven and a dervish in hell.

He asked, "What caused this? It is the opposite of what I thought would happen."

A cry answered him, saying, "The king is in heaven because he associated with dervishes, and the dervish is in hell because he associated with kings."

> *Of what use are things that make you look special?*
> *Just stay away from evil deeds.*
> *You don't need a fancy hat.*
> *Be a dervish and wear something simple.*

STORY 17

Riding a Camel

A BAREFOOT AND BAREHEADED MAN joined our caravan from the city of
Kufah in Iraq to the Hejaz.[14] He would strut back and forth saying:

> *I am neither riding a camel nor loaded down like a camel.*
> *I am neither a lord I nor the vassal of a lord.*
> *I don't crave possessions or regret my past.*
> *I breathe easily and thus spend my life.*

A rich man on a camel called out to him. "O' dervish, where are you
going? Turn back now or you will die." The barefoot man paid him no
attention and continued on.

When they reached Mahmud's oasis, the rich man died. The bare-
foot man, who was sitting next to the rich man's bedroll said, "I didn't
die of hardship by walking, but you certainly died riding on a camel."

> *Someone spent the night weeping over a sick person.*
> *At dawn he died while the sick person lived.*
> *Many fast horses died on the trail,*
> *While slow donkeys finished their journeys alive,*
> *We buried many healthy people,*
> *While sick people keep on living.*

---

14 The Hejaz is the part of Arabia where Mecca is located.

Poison

A HERMIT WAS INVITED TO visit a king. He thought that if he took a little poison he would look gaunt and thereby enhance the king's opinion of him. Unfortunately, he took too much poison and died.

> *I thought he was like a pistachio,*
>> *With a big seed in the middle.*
> *He was really like an onion,*
>> *With one layer on top of another*
> *And nothing inside.*
>> *If a holy man tries to please people*
> *He is praying with his back to the Ka'aba.[15]*
>> *If a worshiper calls upon God,*
> *Then he should focus on God*
>> *And nothing else.*

---

15 In other words, he is praying in the wrong direction.

The Land of Greece

A CARAVAN WAS ROBBED IN the land of Greece, and priceless riches were taken.

The merchants cried and wailed asking God and his prophet to intercede, but it was worthless.

> *When an evil bandit is successful*
> *What does he care if his victims weep?*

Luqman the Wise[16] was in that caravan. Someone asked him, "Could you speak to the robbers and advise them to return some of our treasure because it would be terrible to loose so much?"

He answered, "It would be terrible to speak a word of wisdom to them."

> *Rust which has eaten into iron,*
> *Cannot be removed by polishing.*
> *Why speak to someone with a black heart?*
> *You cannot drive a nail into rock.*

---

16 In Islamic tradition, Luqman is the wisest of men. An entire chapter of the *Qur'an* is devoted to him.

"Actually, it was our mistake." he said.

> *In time of prosperity give aid to the poor,*
>> *A poor man's mind has the power to avert disaster.*
> *When a beggar moans and asks for something,*
>> *Give it.*
> *Otherwise someone might take it by force.*

STORY 20

Music

EVEN THOUGH THE GREAT SHEIKH Abu al Faraj Ibn Jawzi constantly told me to avoid musical gatherings and seek solitude and retirement, the fervor of youth overcame me.

My sensual desires were excited. I headed off in a direction contrary to the advice of my teacher, going to musical events and parties.

When I remembered my sheikh's advice, I would say.

If the qazi[17] were sitting with us,
   He would clap his hands.
If the muhtasib[18] were drinking,
   He would excuse a drunkard.

This went on until I visited a group of people one night.

Among them I saw this musician.

You would have said that his flat-pick
   Was ripping the veins of your arm.

---

17 The word "*qazi*" refers to an Islamic religious judge. As the *Qur'an* forbids the drinking of alcoholic beverages, a *qazi* would be expected to object to drinking wine.

18 The word "*muhtasib*" refers to Islamic religious police.

His voice was worse than the wailing
  Of someone who lost his father.

The people would sometimes put their fingers in their ears. Other times they would put their fingers to their lips motioning for him to stop his singing.

You do not see anyone enjoying your music,
  Until time to go, when you stop playing.
When that musician started to sing
  I told the host, "For God's sake,
Put quicksilver in my ears so I won't hear,
  Or open the door so I can leave."

In short, I tried to please my friends and endured the whole night.

The muezzin[19] has called out at the wrong time,
  Not knowing how much of the night has passed.
Ask what time it is from my eyelids,
  For sleep did not enter my eyes for a moment.

In the morning I took off my turban, pulled a coin from my pocket, and put both before the musician, whom I also embraced and thanked.

My friends saw me thanking the musician and thought I must be crazy. One of them loosened his tongue and began to hassle me saying that I had done something stupid by giving my turban to the singer who had never before gotten a coin in his hand or anything of value placed on his drum[20].

---

19   The word "*muezzin*" refers to the man who calls Muslims to prayer.
20   The custom was to place money or valuables on the drum of a street musician (If you liked the music.).

A musician, may he go far, far away!,
Whom they never see twice in the same place.
As soon as lyrics come out of his mouth,
The hairs on people's bodies stand on end.
Birds on the roof fly away in fear,
He drives us to distraction and tears up his throat.

I said, "It would be wiser for you to hold your tongue, since this musician has done me a great service."

He then asked me to explain in order that he and his friends might understand and apologize for the jokes they had been cracking.

I replied, "Even though my sheikh has often advised me to avoid musical gatherings, I did not listen. Tonight, a lucky star and good fortune have led me to this place, and by means of this musician I have repented and will never again attend such a musical event."

A good voice from a sweet throat, mouth and lips,
Will enchant the heart whether singing or not.
But the music of Khorasan or of Hejaz are not beautiful,
When coming out of a bad singer's throat.

STORY 21

Manners

THEY ASKED LUQMAN, "WHERE DID you learn your manners?"

He answered, "I learn from people who have no manners. Every time I see them doing something distasteful, I know what to avoid."

Telling a joke is a lesson,
   To a wise person.
A fool listens to a hundred chapters of wisdom
   And thinks they are jokes.

Food

IT IS SAID THAT AN ascetic ate ten portions of food and recited the entire *Qur'an* in one night. A wise man heard of this and said, "It would have been better if he had eaten one portion of food and slept the night."

> *Don't fill your guts with food,*
> > *If you want to see the light of wisdom.*
> *You lack wisdom,*
> > *Because you stuffed yourself.*

Perfection

GOD'S MERCY WAS LIKE A lamp that guided a lost sinner until he joined a group of mystics. Blessed by his association with dervishes and influenced by their righteousness, his vices were transformed into virtues. But the tongues of his detractors wagged, saying that, "Nothing has changed. This man's new-found virtue is just a passing fad."

> *Repentance can save you from the wrath of God,*
> *But you can't escape the tongues of men.*

He could not stand his critics, so he asked the elder of the mystics, who answered by saying, "You should be more thankful that you are actually a better person than they think."

> *How long, do you say,*
> *The malevolent and envious will criticize?*
> *Either they get up to shed my blood,*
> *Or they sit down to curse me.*
> *Being good and criticized is better*
> *Than being bad and complimented.*

However, look at me (Saadi) whom everyone thinks is perfection itself. While I worry and think of myself as imperfection.

> *If I really did what I say,*
>> *I would be a righteous ascetic.*
> *I am hidden from my neighbor's eyes,*
>> *God knows what I show and my inner self.*
> *We shut our doors,*
>> *So our faults won't be publicized.*
> *A closed door is useless,*
>> *When God knows all things.*

STORY 24

Defamation

I COMPLAINED TO ONE OF the sheikhs that someone was defaming my character. He answered, "Shame him with your righteous deeds."

> *Be so well behaved,*
>> *That your enemies can't malign you.*
> *If a guitar makes good music,*
>> *The musician will not get angry.*

The Sheikh of Syria

THEY ASKED A SHEIKH FROM Syria, "What is the truth about Sufism?"

He answered, "They were a group scattered over the world, but inwardly united. Now they appear outwardly to be united. But inwardly they are scattered."

If your heart wanders,
　　When you are alone,
You will never experience tranquility.
　　If you have land, respect, farms and goods
And your heart is with God,
　　You are tranquil.

The Fool

I HAVE A MEMORY OF traveling all night in a caravan and falling asleep at dawn next to a thicket. A fool, who had been traveling with us, started whooping and ran out into the wilderness without a moment's rest. The next morning, I asked him what was going on.

"I saw that nightingales were beginning to sing in the trees and quails in the mountains and frogs in the water and beasts in the forest," he said. "I thought it wasn't right that all of them were praising God while I ignored them and slept."

> *Last night a bird was crying in pain.*
> *It upset me so much I couldn't endure it.*
> *One of my most sincere friends*
> *Heard me crying.*
> *He said, "I didn't think a bird's cry*
> *Would upset you so much."*
> *I said, "It's not human for me to stay quiet,*
> *While a bird praises God."*

The Oasis of Bani Hilal

ONE TIME I WAS ON a trip to Hejaz accompanied by a group of dervishes who were masters of their hearts.[21] They frequently sang and recited mystical poems. A devotee was also on this journey.

He didn't understand the mystical states of dervishes, or the pain they carried in their hearts.

When we arrived at the oasis of Bani Hilal, a child came running out of an encampment of Arabs. He sang so beautifully, that the birds came to hear him. I saw the devotee's camel begin to dance. It threw the man off its back and ran away.

"Oh sheikh," I said to the man. "The child's singing had a profound effect on the camel, but it did nothing for you."

> Do you know what the nightingale
>   Said to me at dawn?
> "Who are you
>   That love means nothing?"
> The Arab's poetry
>   Made the camels dance and sing,
> If you have no desire,

---

21 See the introduction for an explanation of "master of heart" and "devotee."

Then you are strange.
Everything you see
    Calls out in recognition of God.
A heart that can listen
    Knows this.
The nightingale on the rose bush sings praises,
    Even the thorns sing out to God.

The Beggar King

A KING'S LIFE HAD COME to an end, and he had no successor. He stipulated in his will that the first person to come through the city gate after he died would be crowned the next king.[22]

By chance, the first person to come through the gate was a man in tattered clothing and who spent his entire life begging for morsels. The old king's ministers and nobles did what he stipulated and presented the beggar with the keys to the old king's fortress and treasure houses.

The beggar ruled the kingdom for a while until some princes rebelled. This threw the country into strife. All of the nobles deployed their soldiers, and things went out of control.

The poor man was worried about what was going on until a friend, whom he had known when he was with the dervishes, came to see him.

"Thank God, the Merciful and Compassionate," said the friend. "Who has brought the beggar's body and his feet from the thorns? You have been guided by luck, and good fortune has brought you here.

---

22 A similar story appears in the *Arabian Nights* as part of the tale of An Nadir and Zimrud. In the *Arabian Nights* version, Zimrud comes to a city disguised as a man. In the city, the people proclaim her king and tell her the previous king decreed before dying that the first person to come through the city gates after his death should be the new king.

Sometimes a flower blooms.
Sometimes it withers.
Sometimes a tree is barren.
Sometimes it bears fruit."

"My dear friend," the beggar said. "Console me because this is no place for congratulations. When you last saw me I was worried about getting enough bread. Now I worry about the entire land."

We hurt if we are not rich.
If we are, the wealth traps us.
Wealth is the greatest of problems.
Whether we have it or not.
If you want wealth, seek contentment.
Only that is blessed wealth.
If a rich man gives you gold,
He is only helping himself.
I have often heard from the great ones,
That a dervish's patience is greater,
Than a rich man's generosity.
If Bahram roasts an onager[23],
It is not like a locust leg from an ant.

---

23 An onager is a wild donkey.

The Royal Court

A MAN HAD A FRIEND who worked in the royal court. He hadn't seen him for a while. Someone said, "You haven't seen him for a long time."

He answered, "I don't want to see him."

It happened that a member of the court was present. He asked, "What did he do wrong?"

"He didn't do anything wrong." Said the man, "It is best to see friends from the court after they've been discharged. Otherwise, he will be pained to see me."[24]

> The great ones who work in the court
>> Spend free time away from companions.
> The day they're discharged and powerless
>> They bring their heart ache to friends.

---

24 The implication being that if you visit a friend in the court, you will be asking for some kind of favor.

Abu Hurayra

ABU HURAYRA[25] WOULD SEE THE Holy Prophet every day.

The Holy Prophet said, "Don't come every day so you will be appreciated more."

A master of his heart, was told that even though the sun shines every day, no one has ever fallen in love with it or made it a friend. He replied, "That is because you can see it every day, except it winter when it is hidden. Then you desire it."

> *It's not a bad idea to visit people.*
> *Don't go so often they tell you to stop.*
> *You can complain about yourself.*
> *Don't make others complain about you.*

---

25 Abu Hurayra was a follower and personal friend of the Prophet Muhammad. He was known for preserving and relating a number of stories about the Prophet (*Hadith*) and is frequently quoted by Islamic jurists and scholars.

Guts

ONE OF THE GREAT ONES' guts began to gurgle with gas. He couldn't control it, and he farted.

"My friends," he said. "I couldn't control what happened. No one has accused me of a crime, and I feel relieved. Please forgive me."

> *Your guts are a prison for gas*
> > *But gas cannot be imprisoned.*
> *When gas gurgles in the guts, let it out.*
> > *Gas in the guts is a burden on the heart.*
> *When someone acts surly and tries to leave,*
> > *Don't hold him back.*

Slavery

I GOT TIRED OF SOCIALIZING with my friends in Damascus. So I headed for the desert around Jerusalem and made friends with the wild animals until I got captured by the crusaders. They took me to Tripoli and put me to work in a ditch along with some Jews.

One of the chiefs from Aleppo, whom I already knew, passed by one day.

He recognized me.

"Hey friend, what's going on?" he said.

"What can I say?" I replied.

> *I fled from civilization into the wilderness,*
> *So no one would distract me from God.*
> *Compare that to where I am now,*
> *Making do in a stable full of people.*
> *It's better to have chains on your feet among friends,*
> *Than to be in a garden with strangers.*

He felt compassion for me, so he paid the crusaders ten dinars and took me back to Aleppo. There, he married me off to one of his daughters and gave me a hundred dinars as a dowry.

Some time passed. The woman was bad tempered, spiteful and rejecting. She began to nag me, and our love was finished.

> *A bad woman in a good man's house is like hell on earth.*
> *Beware a bad woman, beware!*

"Aren't you the one my father ransomed from the crusaders?" she would taunt me.

"Yes," I said, "For ten dinars he bought me from captivity by the crusaders, and for a hundred dinars he put me in your hands."

> *I heard that a great man*
> *Saved a sheep from a wolf.*
> *That night he put a knife to its throat,*
> *The sheep wailed,*
> *"You saved me from the wolf's claws,*
> *Now I see that you yourself*
> *Are a wolf."*

STORY 33

Expenses

ONE OF THE KINGS ASKED a devotee how he spent his time.

"All night I pray to God," he answered. "All day I am a slave to expenses."

The king understood what the devotee was talking about. He ordered his people to give regular payments to the devotee and ease the burden on his heart.

> *O provider, whose feet are tied by family,*
>> *You will never rest again.*
> *Worry about children, bread, food, sustenance,*
>> *Will bring you back from traveling the heavens.*
> *I am busy all day,*
>> *So at night I can be with God.*
> *All night I pray,*
>> *So my children will eat tomorrow.*

The Ascetic

IN SYRIA, THERE WAS A pious ascetic who lived in the forest and survived by eating the leaves off trees. A king, who was passing through the area, went to visit him.

"If it is all right with you," the king said. "I will build you a place in the city so it will be easier for you to pray. Also, other people will be able to benefit from the blessing of your spirit and by imitating your pious behavior."

The ascetic didn't like the king's suggestion, so he turned his face away.

"Make the king happy by coming to the city for a few days," one of the king's ministers said. "See if it is worth your time. Later on, if other people bother you, you can do what you want."

The ascetic went into the city, where the king's own garden was set up for him. It was a delightful, restful place.

> *Its red roses were like the cheeks of beautiful women.*
> *Its hyacinths were like hair of the most beloved,*
> *Not old and plundered by the cold of winter,*
> *Like a wet nurse, whose milk no child has drunk.*

Then the king sent the ascetic a beautiful maiden.

A face beautiful as the moon and glorious as a peacock to steal
    The ascetic's mind,
Upon seeing her the ascetic's body would not be capable of
    Forbearance.

Then, after the maiden, the king sent a slave boy who was extraordinarily handsome.

No one could watch him enough.
    It was like trying to drink a river.

The ascetic began to eat fine food and wear fine clothing. He ate fruit, melons and candy while looking at the slave boy and the maiden. The wise ones have said that the hair of beautiful people chains the mind and snares clever birds.

With complete awareness I put my heart and faith
    In your service.
Today I am the clever bird and you are the snare.

To make a long story short, the wealth of virtue that the ascetic had developed over a long time was dissipated.

The poet has said,

Anyone who is a judge, or an elder, or a disciple,
    And who is free from scandal.
If he comes down into the world of temptation,
    It is as if a fly gets stuck in honey.

Once again, the king wanted to see the ascetic. He saw that the ascetic had changed. Where once he was all red and healthy, now he was all pale and had grown fat. He was reclining on brocade pillows while the slave boy waved a fan of peacock feathers over him. They talked about all sorts of things.

"There are two groups of people that I love more than anyone," the king said. "They are scholars and ascetics."

One of the king's ministers was a philosopher and a world watcher.

"Your majesty, a sign of your friendship with these two groups is that you do good to them," the minister said. "Give gold to the scholars so they can study more. Give nothing to the ascetics so that they may continue to be ascetics."

> *Tell a beautiful woman not to wear makeup or wear turquoise*
>   *Rings.*
> *Tell a dervish who is good and pure not to eat free food or go*
>   *Begging.*
> *As long as I have and need more, don't call me an ascetic.*

The Pledge

ONCE, A KING WAS DEALING with a problem.

He said, "If this situation ends the way I want, I will give money to the ascetics."

When the problem resolved itself, and the king stopped worrying, it was time to fulfill his pledge. He gave a bag of coins to one of his trusted servants and told him to go give it to the ascetics.

The servant, who was both clever and wise, went about day and night with the money looking for ascetics. He finally came back and told the king that he couldn't find any.

The king said, "What are you telling me? I know for a fact that there are four hundred ascetics in this country."

"Your majesty," the servant replied. "If they are truly ascetics, they don't want the money. If they want the money, they aren't really ascetics."

The king finally told his servants, "Even though it is right to worship God with devotion and humility, this joke made me angry. However, the truth is on the side of this servant."

The king dropped the matter.

> *If an ascetic takes cash from you,*
> > *Go find someone more ascetic.*
> *Someone who acts well and is close to God*
> > *Without getting handouts or charity.*
> *A beautiful finger or a charming earlobe are lovely*
> > *Without jewelry or rings.*

Charity

THEY ASKED AN ESTABLISHED MEMBER of the *ulema*[26], "What do you say about charity food?"

He said, "If you take charity food because you are in need, it is permitted. If people gather just to get food, it is forbidden."

> *Wise people take food to help their devotions.*
> *They don't practice devotions to take food.*

---

26 The word "*ulema*" refers to scholars of *sha'aria* or Muslim law.

The Dinner Party

A DERVISH ENTERED A HOUSE belonging to a person who was generous and wise. The homeowner was entertaining a group of educated and kind people. Every one of them told a joke or a funny story as was the custom of sophisticated people. The dervish had just crossed the desert, so he was exhausted and had not eaten.

One of the guests, by way of polite conversation, said to the dervish, "You should say something too."

The dervish said, "I am not funny and do not know literature like these others, and I have not read anything interesting recently. So, you will have to be satisfied with one little verse of poetry from me."

"Say it," they all replied.

The dervish recited,

I am hungry and sitting before a table cloth covered with food.
Like a bachelor in front of the door to the women's bath.

The guests all laughed and praised the dervish's verse. Then the food was brought in. The host said, "Wait a moment. My servants will be bringing in some *kufteh kababs*."[27]

The dervish raised his head and said, "There doesn't need to be meat at my table, for a hungry man bread is as good as *kufteh kababs*."

---

27 *"Kufteh kababs"* are skewers of roasted ground meat.

Give and Take

A DISCIPLE ASKED HIS TEACHER. "What should I do? People come to see me all the time. It's confusing, and it upsets me."

The teacher answered. "Give money to the ones who are true dervishes. Ask for money from the ones who are rich. If you do that, people won't come to bother you anymore."

> *If the army of Islam consisted of a single beggar,*
>> *Then the infidels would flee to China to escape his asking*
>>> *For handouts.*

The Mediator

A MAN WHO MEDIATED IN disputes said to his father, "The colorful, attractive words of people don't affect me, because they do not follow their own advice.

> *"They advise people to give up the world,*
> *While they collect silver and food.*
> *The scholar who only talks about what should be.*
> *His words will have no effect on anyone.*
> *The scholar should not do badly himself.*
> *Not someone who talks and does not do.*

'Do you tell people to be righteous and forget it yourselves...?'[28]

> *A scholar who is successful yet indulges himself is lost.*
> *Whom can he guide?"*

The father said, "O' son!

---

28 This refers to a verse from the *Qur'an*, which says. "Do you tell people to be righteous and forget it yourselves? Though you read the Book you have no sense." *Qur'an* (2:44) The "Book" in this case refers to the *Qur'an* itself.

"Not for idle thought should you turn away from instruction,
    Assume the learned are in error,
Or search unendingly for the perfect scholar.
    Like the blind man who slipped in the mud,
And called on all Muslims to bring him a lamp.
    A nearby prostitute saw him and said,
'You can't even see the lamp!
    What will you see with it?'
A prayer meeting is like a fabric store.
    There, if you don't produce cash,
You don't get materials.
    Here, if you don't have devotion,
You will not find happiness.
    Listen to the scholar with the ear of your soul,
Even if he doesn't practice as he preaches.
    People who make false claims are themselves false.
How can one who is asleep wake another?
    A man must know himself to hear,
Even if the advice is written on a wall."

A man, who was master of his own heart, broke his promise to stay with the Sufis. He came to a religious school.

I asked him,

> *"What is the difference between Sufis and scholars?*
> *Since you left one group and joined the other."*

He said,

> *"One tries to save his own carpet from a flood.*
> *The other tries to save drowning people."*

The Drunkard

A MAN WAS LYING IN the street, so drunk he couldn't control his limbs. An ascetic passed by and stared at the man in his condition. The young man raised his head and in his intoxicated state said. "When they pass that which is vain, they pass with nobility."[29]

> *If you see one who sins, be silent and forgive.*
> > *You who disapprove, why not pass with nobility?*
> *Ascetic, don't turn your head from a sinner.*
> > *Look at him with forgiveness.*
> *If I act in a disrespectful manner,*
> > *You should still pass me with respect.*

---

29 The full verse is, "And those who do not bear witness to falsehood, when they pass by that which is vain, they pass with nobility." *Qur'an* (25:72).

The Robe

A GROUP OF ROBBERS ENTERED the home of a dervish, insulted him and beat him up. Upset, he went to the elder of his order and told him what happened. "My son," said the elder. "That patched dervish's robe, which you are wearing, is a symbol of happiness. Anyone who is not willing to endure hardship has no claim to wear that robe."

A stone thrown in the water will not disturb the deep sea.
The mystic who gets offended is really shallow.
Be like the dust that your body will someday become.
Be forgiving and become pure.

The Flag and The Veil

HEAR THIS STORY, AN ARGUMENT between a flag and a veil.

The flag, covered with dust from the road and sore from the stirrups, said this to the veil by way of reproach.

> *"You and I are both eunuchs, servants at the sultan's court.*
>> *I never rest. Time and time again I travel.*
> *You have never felt the pain of being tested.*
>> *You have never seen forts, or deserts, wind or dust.*
> *My feet have advanced by effort.*
>> *So why do you have greater honor?*
> *You lie upon affectionate concubines,*
>> *With slave boys that smell of jasmine.*
> *I have fallen into the hands of soldiers,*
>> *A prisoner of soldiers traveling by foot."*

The veil answered,

> *"I have my head on the threshold,*
>   *Not like you, who has his head in the sky.*
> *Anyone who stretches his neck out*
>   *Gets his head cut off."*

The Weightlifter

A MAN, WHO WAS MASTER of his own heart, saw a weightlifter who was very upset, sitting with his head in his hands.

He asked what was going on, and people told him that someone had insulted the weightlifter.

They said, "This fool can lift a thousand pounds, but he cannot bear harsh words."

> *Do not make claims and boast of fighting skill.*
> *A weak soul is vile, be it male or female.*
> *If you have power, sweeten people's mouths.*
> *A fist in the mouth is not manliness.*
> *Even if he can break apart an elephant's forehead,*
> *A man is no man without kindness.*
> *The children of Adam are made of dirt.*
> *Be humble like the earth, or you are not a man.*

The Brethren of Purity

I ASKED A GREAT MAN about what the "brethren of purity" did.

He said, "They put the wishes of their friends above their own."

The wise ones have said, "A brother who thinks only of himself is neither a brother nor truly in control of himself."

> *If your traveling companion rushes, you stop.*
> *Do not give your heart to one who doesn't give his*
> *Heart to you.*
> *When someone is neither righteous nor pious,*
> *Cutting him off is better than remaining loyal.*

I remember that someone who did not like me criticized what I said in this verse, saying that the *Qur'an* forbids cutting off family members, and that you should have affection for relatives. I told him it agreed with the *Qur'an*, "And if they contend with you and say you should associate with me something of which you have no knowledge, do not obey them."[30]

> *A thousand relatives who are strangers to God should be*
> *Sacrificed to one relative who is close.*

---

30   The full verse is, "And if they contend with you and say you should associate with Me something of which you have no knowledge, do not obey them and live with them in this world with kindness, and follow the path of one who turns to Me, to Me is your return, for I will tell you what you did." (*Qur'an* 31:15). This verse says one should not take foolish words seriously. At the same time, one should, "live with them in this world with kindness."

The Cobbler

A nice, but gullible old man married his daughter to a
*   Cobbler.*
On the wedding night, the brute bit the daughter's lip so
*   Badly it bled.*
The next morning the father saw her and asked the cobbler,
*   Why he did such a boorish thing to his daughter.*
"I'm not joking," He said. "I'm being serious.
*   Your behavior shows you to be a brute. Let her go."*

Ugliness

THERE WAS ONCE A LEARNED man who had an ugly daughter. She had grown up and had a dowry and money, but no one wanted to marry her.

> Silk and brocade look ugly
>> On a woman who is not beautiful.

All things considered, the best thing was to marry her to a blind man.

Then a doctor came from Ceylon who knew how to heal the eyes of those who could not see.

They asked the learned man, "Why don't you have your son-in-law treated?"

"I'm afraid he will get his eyesight back and divorce my daughter," he answered. "It's better if the husband of an ugly woman can't see."

The Path of the Dervishes

A KING LOOKED AT A group of dervishes with contempt. One of the dervishes got up and wisely said to the king,

"O' King, in this world we mean less to you than soldiers, but we are happier. In death we are equal, and with regards to resurrection, we are better."

> *If the ruler is prosperous, then the dervish needs bread.*
> *At death, they take nothing from this world but a*
> *Shroud.*
> *When you pack your goods and prepare to leave,*
> *It's better to be a beggar than a king.*

On the outside, dervishes have ragged clothing and unkempt hair. In truth, the dervish on the inside has a heart full of life and a dead spirit (of evil).[31]

> *He won't sue.*
> *If opposed he won't fight.*
> *But if a millstone rolls down a hillside,*
> *He will duck out of its way.*

The path of the dervishes is one of remembering(*dhikr*)[32], gratitude(*shukr*), service(*khadimat*)[33], worship(*tauat*)[34], generosity(*ithiyar*), contentment(*qanaat*)[35], proclaming unity(*tawheed*)[36], trust in God(*tawwakul*), submission(*taslim*)[37] and forbearance(*tahammul*)[38]. Anyone who can be descrbed by the qualities I have told you is a dervish even if he wears fine clothing. On the other hand, if someone is licentious(*harze kardi*), does not pray, lusts, capricious(*havaparsat*), impulsive(*hush baz*) during the day and spends the night living in dreams(*ghafat*)[39], eats whatever he wants and says whatever he wants, is a fool even if he looks like a dervish.

---

31 Sufi philosophy talks of two kinds of sprit, the *nafs-e-khub* or good spirit and the *nafs-e-shaitan* or spirit of evil. Sufis engage in various spiritual practices designed to destroy the spirit of evil within them.

32 *Dhikr* in this context refers to types of chants and meditations practiced by Sufis.

33 *Khadimat*, acting as a servant of God.

34 *Tauat*, keeping a promise. In this case, it refers to Muslim religious practice.

35 *Qanaat*, to be satisfied with the bare necessities.

36 *Tawheed*, proclaiming the unity of God. *Tawheed* can also refer to promoting unity in general, like organizing people into one group or working together in harmony.

37 *Taslim* comes from the same root as the word *Muslim*. It means to voluntarily submit to God's will.

38 *Tahammul*, to be strong enough to accept what is hard for you.

39 *Ghafat* can also mean being amoral or a glutton.

Don't hang a fine curtain in your window,
  If you have cheap matting in your house.

Roses Among The Weeds

I saw some roses growing
    Among a clump of weeds.
I said, "What are these weeds
    Doing with roses."
The weeds cried and said, "Be quiet.
    Companionship doesn't detract from nobility.
Even though I have no beauty, color or smell,
    Am I not a plant in God's garden?
I am the servant of a bountiful lord,
    Nourished by his generosity.
Whether or not I possess virtue,
    I hope for grace from God.
Although I have no possessions,
    No skills to offer.
God knows what to give
    To a slave who can do no more.
The tradition is to free
    The slave who is old."

O' God, who decorates the world,
*   Be generous with an old servant,*
Saadi, choose the way to the Ka'aba.
*   O' man of God, find the door to God.*
Unlucky is he who turns away
*   From this door. There is no other.*

STORY 49

Generosity Or Courage

THEY ASKED A WISE MAN, "Which is better, generosity or courage?"

He answered, "One who has generosity has no need of courage."

> *Hatim Tayi exists no more,*
>> *But he will always be renowned for goodness.*
> *Donate from your wealth,*
>> *A pruned grape vine yields better grapes.*
> *It is written on the grave of Bahram Gor,*
>> *A noble hand is better than a powerful arm*

Printed in Great Britain
by Amazon